ESCAPE!
The Life of Harry Houdini

Illustrated with photographs

ESCAPE!

The Life of
Harry Houdini

by FLORENCE MEIMAN WHITE

Julian Messner New York

Photo Credits
Library of Congress: pp. 2, 8, 36, 44, 52, 63, 68,
71, 73, 76, 80, 86, 87, 91, 93, 96, 99, 103
New York Public Library Picture Collection: pp. 17,
25, 48
Wide World Photos: pp. 33, 59

Manufactured in the United States of America

Design by Sheila Lynch

Library of Congress Cataloging in Publication Data

White, Florence Meiman, 1910-
Escape! : The Life of Harry Houdini.

SUMMARY: Highlights the life and career of one of the
world's greatest escape artists and magicians.
[1.   Houdini, Harry, 1874-1926.   2. Magicians]
1.   Houdini, Harry, 1874-1926—Juvenile literature.
2.   Magicians—United States—Biography—Juvenile
literature.   I.   Title.
GV1545.H8W47   793.8'092'4   [B]   [92]   78-26248
ISBN 0-671-32937-5

To Andrew and Stephen,
and
to All the Girls and Boys in the World
Who Want to Be Magicians
with Love
and Best Wishes

Books by Florence M. White

Escape! The Life of Harry Houdini
Malcolm X
Cesar Chavez
How to Lose Your Best Friend
How to Lose Your Lunch Money
Your Friend, the Tree
Your Friend, the Insect
One Boy Lives in My House
My House Is the Nicest Place

Contents

A portrait of Harry Houdini at the height of his fame.

1

Starting Out

"I'm telling you, Jack. One year from now I'll be the best magician in New York — in America — in the whole world!" The handsome young man with the black curly hair threw back his shoulders. Because he was only five feet eight inches, he always held his head high to seem taller. Now he held it a little higher as he spoke to his friend. His English was bad. He had learned to speak it on the street. In his home, the family spoke Yiddish or German.

It was 1891. Ehrich Weiss, age 17, had just left his job as a necktie cutter in New York City to become Harry Houdini, professional magician.

Ehrich Weiss was born on March 24, 1874, in Budapest, Hungary. The Budapest city government has a record of his birth. But Harry Houdini claimed that he was born on April 6, 1874, in Appleton, Wisconsin. He said his mother had told

---

1

Starting Out

"I'm telling you, Jack. One year from now I'll be the best magician in New York — in America — in the whole world!" The handsome young man with the black curly hair threw back his shoulders. Because he was only five feet eight inches, he always held his head high to seem taller. Now he held it a little higher as he spoke to his friend. His English was bad. He had learned to speak it on the street. In his home, the family spoke Yiddish or German.

It was 1891. Ehrich Weiss, age 17, had just left his job as a necktie cutter in New York City to become Harry Houdini, professional magician.

Ehrich Weiss was born on March 24, 1874, in Budapest, Hungary. The Budapest city government has a record of his birth. But Harry Houdini claimed that he was born on April 6, 1874, in Appleton, Wisconsin. He said his mother had told

9

him so. With a mind for changing things around, Harry found it easy to make himself believe that he was born in the United States.

Shortly after Ehrich was born, his father, Rabbi Samuel Weiss, left Hungary for the United States. Hungarian friends who had settled in the small city of Appleton helped him find a position as a rabbi there. His wife Cecilia and their four small boys, Herman, Nathan, William, and Ehrich, followed soon after. Rabbi Weiss was a scholar, a man of learning. He spoke Hungarian, Hebrew, Yiddish, and German. But he found it hard to learn English and to adjust to the ways of his new country. As a result, he soon had to leave his position.

The family had become larger with the arrival of Theodore and Leopold, but Rabbi Weiss's earnings had become less. At eight years of age, Ehrich and his older brothers began to shine shoes and to sell newspapers to help support the family.

Cecilia Weiss did the best she could with the money she had. She was proud of her educated husband. When he sat down to read his books of Jewish learning, she sent their lively and noisy children outside to play in the backyard.

On cold winter days, she baked cakes for the children. Ehrich loved the sweet smells of cinnamon, raisins, and apples that the cakes sent off.

He loved eating these delicious cakes, too. He could finish an entire cake by himself.

"Ehrich, you must leave some for the other children," his mother scolded him lovingly, as she saw him inching toward the cupboard door one day. After many such lectures did no good, she put a lock on the cupboard. But her Ehrich soon found a way to open it. He was good with locks even as a little boy.

When he was in the fourth grade, Ehrich left school and went to work in a locksmith's shop. In 1883 many children worked in shops and factories. There were no laws that forced children to go to school.

He learned that one key could open many locks. He discovered that he could make lock-picks from small pieces of wire. He was soon able to open every lock in the shop. One winter night when there was no one on the street, he opened the lock of every shop on the block. The next morning the angry shopkeepers complained to his boss. Ehrich never tried such mischief again.

At home, Ehrich liked to balance himself like a tight rope walker on a thick clothesline that stretched between two trees in the backyard. He also practiced acrobatics on a home-made trapeze that hung from a tree. No one practiced anything as much as Ehrich. Whatever he did had to be

11

perfect. "You're good, Ehrich," the other boys admitted without really wanting to.

When a circus came to Appleton, nine-year-old Ehrich got a job as an acrobat for 35 cents a week. He wore long red stockings to look like the tights of a real acrobat. The young performer called himself "Prince of the Air."

"Would you like to see a magic show, Ehrich?" his father asked shortly after the circus left town. "I have to go to Milwaukee. A famous magician will be there."

"Sure, Pa, sure." The nine-year-old gulped. He was almost too surprised to speak. In a poor family such treats were rare.

At the theater, Ehrich stared, his mouth wide open, as the magician cut up a man — first an arm, then a leg, then the head. Until the man was put together again, Ehrich cauld hardly breath. How did he do it? He wondered all the way home. He often thought about that show as he worked in the locksmith's shop.

When Ehrich was twelve his father took him aside to talk about an important matter. "My son," he said in a serious tone, "I know I can depend on you. Promise that if anything ever happens to me, you will always take care of Mama." The father had more confidence in Ehrich than in his other sons. Ehrich worked hard and always kept his promises. Rabbi Weiss placed a thick book on the table in front of Ehrich. It was the Torah, the holy Jewish law. With his right hand on the Torah, the boy promised he would always take care of his mother.

Now Ehrich felt a great responsibility for his family. He had to make something of himself, to do something big.

But he felt he couldn't do it in Appleton.

Early one morning in the spring of 1886, young Ehrich Weiss sneaked out of his house and headed for the open road. Along the way he mailed a note to his mother. "Dear Ma," the note read, "I am going to Galveston, Texas and will be home in about a year. My best regards to all. Your truant son, Ehrich Weiss."

Traveling on foot and on freight trains, he earned his food by washing dishes in restaurants and picking crops on farms. He slept in barns and fields.

One day Ehrich received a letter from his mother while working at a farm. "Your father has gone to New York. Maybe it will be easier for him to find work there." She said that she and the other children would be joining Rabbi Weiss soon.

Ehrich read the letter several times.

New York! Ehrich thought. The greatest city in the world! The place to find fame, fortune, excitement, anything and everything that an ambitious boy wanted. Famous people were there and theaters and the Barnum and Bailey Circus and Coney Island.

It was 1888. Ehrich caught a freight train bound for New York.

2

New York, New York

Ehrich found his father living in a boarding house and teaching in a small Jewish school. After Ehrich got a job as a messenger for a department store, the father and son rented a three-room apartment in a tenement building on East 69th Street. They saved every penny they could for railroad fare for Mama and the children. Herman, the oldest boy, had died. Now there were Nathan and William, his two older brothers, and Theo and Leopold, his two younger ones.

Ehrich had not seen the family for more than a year. He could hardly wait for them to arrive. Soon the apartment was filled with talk and laughter and quarrels — and the cries of a new-born sister, Cari Gladys, the only girl among the Weiss children. It was crowded in the three small rooms near the East River. Because tenements were built close to each other, there was little light and air.

"The river's a swell place to go swimming when it's hot," Ehrich told his delighted brothers.

"And best of all, we're all together," Mama said as she hugged Ehrich to her breast. "Never run away again, my son."

One night Ehrich came home from the department store with mischief in his eyes. "Shake me," he instructed his mother. Mrs. Weiss shook him. The tips he had received that day flew out of his hair, ears, and sleeves. Mother and son laughed as they picked up the precious coins from the floor.

When Ehrich was fourteen, he took a job as an assistant necktie cutter in Richter's necktie factory. He earned about $3 a week. This was more than he was making as a messenger in the department store. Jacob Hayman worked alongside him at the cutting table.

Jacob, or Jack, as Ehrich called him, was also interested in magic and always carried a pack of cards in his pocket. During their short lunch break, the two boys taught each other tricks as they gulped down the sandwiches they had brought from home.

At night Jacob took Ehrich to magic shops. Ehrich saw tricks so wonderful he could hardly believe they were possible. They were expensive, too expensive for him. But in the cheap second-hand bookshops in his neighborhood, he found books on magic that sold for a nickel. If the books were torn a bit, they were sometimes even cheaper.

One night Ehrich picked up an old book. The cover was so faded he could barely read the title, "Memoirs of Robert-Houdin, Ambassador, Author and Conjuror." Conjuror? That meant magician. He opened the book and began to read. It was the story of the greatest magician in France. He turned a few pages, read more, then thrust his hand into his pocket and pulled out the few coins he had. Just enough to buy the book. There would be no

Robert Houdin, the magician from whom Harry Houdini got his name.

money left for trolley fare. (A trolley is a street car run on tracks by electricity from a wire strung high above the street.) He made the purchase anyway and hurried out.

In the room he shared with Theo and Leopold, Ehrich lit the gas jet hanging from the ceiling, sat down on his bed and began to read. All night he read, while his brothers tossed about and complained about the light. When his mother came into the room the next morning, Ehrich looked at her with surprise. His mind was still in France. He was imagining Robert-Houdin, the great magician performing in the palace of the king.

It was hard to wait until lunchtime to tell Jacob about his new hero. "Jack, I want to be like Robert-Houdin. I want to become the greatest magician in the world." His voice was serious and forceful.

Jacob Hayman understood. He, too, wanted to become a magician.

"Why not, Ehrich?" he answered. "Just put an 'i' at the end of Houdin. That will mean 'like Houdin.'" Neither boy knew a word of French, but the name sounded wonderful to Ehrich.

"Houdin. Houdini. Harry Houdini." Ehrich said the words slowly. Harry was the name of the famous American magician, Harry Keller. Ehrich had heard of him but had never seen him. Some day, he, too, would be famous, would perform before kings.

In 1890, working hours were long and wages were little. Harry worked ten hours a day, six days a week at the necktie factory. Cutting neckties was dull. But now he had something to dream about. In the little time he had for fun, he joined the Pastime Athletic Club in the neighborhood. He was a thin young man. At the Club he could develop his body and keep in good physical condition. He became a member of the track team. Wearing red satin trunks made by his mother, he ran so well he won a medal. He learned how to swim well. To friends in the club, he made a promise that he would never smoke or drink so that he would maintain his physical fitness.

On April 8, 1891, the night of his seventeenth birthday, Ehrich announced at the family supper table, "I've quit my job. I'm through cutting neckties." All eyes turned to him in surprise. No one in a poor family gave up a steady job, even at $3 a week.

"What are you going to do, Ehrich?" his father asked quietly.

"I'm going into show business," Ehrich answered. His voice was firm, confident. "I'm going to be a magician."

The family's surprise turned to shock. How

could a man make a living from magic? Rabbi Weiss had expected his sons to become scholars, doctors, businessmen. Ehrich could see the disappointment in his father's eyes. Mama Weiss said nothing. She recognized her son's determination. She had been aware of this quality in him ever since he was a small boy. When he undertook something difficult, he worked at it until he was successful. She could rely on him when she needed help. He was always eager to please her. There was a very special affection between this son and his mother.

Ehrich would succeed, she thought to herself. Yes, her Ehrich would succeed at whatever he would do.

3

The Great
Mystery Trunk Escape

Jacob Hayman, Ehrich's co-worker in the factory, had joined him as his partner. Jacob was about the same age as Ehrich. They called themselves "The Houdini Brothers."

"Jack," Ehrich said, thinking only of himself, "one year from now I'm going to be rich and famous." His intense blue-grey eyes were filled with determination — the determination of a young man who could not fail, who would not fail.

Jack was less confident than his new partner. "Sure hope you're right, Ehrich. I mean Harry." He grinned. "I may as well start calling you by your new name if we're going to be professional."

Full of hope, the Houdini Brothers began their search for work. They went to booking agents whose business it was to help show business people get jobs. The agents watched the two young magicians make coins appear and disappear, flip cards that sailed through the room and back, and change a blue silk handkerchief into a pink one.

"We'll call you when we need you," they told the boys as they left.

"No polish, no experience," one agent said to his partner. "You're right," the other answered. "That short Houdini kid with the bushy hair — clumsy with those cards. Can't even speak English well. He'll never get anywhere."

Sometimes the two boys found jobs on their own in beer halls, where the audience was drunk and noisy. Sometimes they entertained at a neighborhood party or club meeting and earned a dollar or two.

After four months of more disappointment than work, Jacob Hayman quit the partnership. Harry took on another partner, his fifteen-year-old brother Theo. The younger boy had been his booster and admirer ever since they were children. In those days, Harry gave acrobatic shows for other kids in the family's backyard. "You sure can do anything, Ehrich," Theo would say with admiration.

When he wasn't job hunting, Harry would spend hours looking around magic shops, longing for tricks he couldn't afford to buy. He would have to stay with the cards and silks, he thought, and the props he could make at home.

One day as Harry and Theo were leaving Martinka's Magic Shop on 6th Avenue, they ran into a magician, down on his luck.

"You interested in buying a trick box?" the man asked.

Harry was always interested in something new. "I sure would like to see it," he answered.

The boys went with the elderly man to his home. In a corner of his room stood a box large enough for a person to get into.

"It's a one-in one-out act," the older magician explained. "One person gets in, the other gets out without the box seeming to have been opened. The trick is to change places quickly." The box came with a sack and a four-sided frame that was surrounded by a black curtain. The magician called it a cabinet. Harry looked carefully at the wooden box and the things that came with it.

"Best trick you'll ever buy, young fellows," the magician urged. "The audience will never guess how you do it. I'll sell it to you for only $25, a bargain at that price."

"Only $25! Where'll we get that much money?" Theo groaned as he and Harry walked home.

"Maybe this trick will help us get work," Harry answered brightly. "It looks like a good one." He thought for a minute. "We're going to borrow the money, Theo. That's what we're going to do."

"From whom?" Theo asked. Most of the people they knew were not much richer than they were.

Harry and Theo spent the next few days visiting relatives and friends. One loaned them $3, another $2. An uncle with a steady job loaned them $10. "I hope you'll make a million dollars with that box, Ehrich," the uncle laughed.

"I will," Harry assured him with a serious voice. "I will. You'll see how soon I will pay you back."

By the following week the boys had borrowed enough to buy the box. That night they stayed up close to midnight. Over and over they practiced getting in and out of the box. It was a little hard for the six-foot tall Theo, but they practiced until they did it perfectly.

"It's great, Theo," Harry said, his eyes gleaming with excitement. "Let's try it out on Mama." They could hear their mother in the kitchen, kneading a challah, a fine white egg-bread for her family to eat on Friday night, the start of the Jewish Sabbath.

"Ma, come in and see our new trick," Harry called out, as he set a chair for his mother in the doorway. "Another new trick, boys? Wait. I'll wipe my hands of the flour." They spoke Yiddish to each other.

Mama Weiss sat down.

"Ladies and Gentlemen," Harry began.

Cecilia Weiss, Harry's mother.

Mama laughed. "I'm not ladies and gentlemen. I'm only Mama." Her merry eyes twinkled.

As Cecilia Weiss looked on, Harry tied Theo's hands behind his back, put him into the sack, knotted it, and placed the sack in the box. He locked the box, tied it from side to side and front to back. Then he placed the cabinet with the black curtain over the box.

"When I clap my hands three times, a miracle will happen," Harry said to his one-woman audience.

Harry clapped, then dashed behind the curtain. Almost at once Theo was in front. He drew open the curtain. Mama could see the box still locked and tied. Harry was nowhere in sight.

"Where's Ehrich?" Mama Weiss said, looking around the small room, wondering how her son had disappeared.

Theo laughed. "Right here, Ma." He untied and unlocked the box. Harry was inside.

They had changed places in less than a minute!

Mama applauded. "Wonderful, children. Wonderful! It's truly a miracle. But how did you do it?"

"It's a secret, Mama," Harry teased. "We are magicians." Mama looked disappointed.

"All right. I'll show you." Harry loved his mother too much to hurt her for even a moment. "Look at this side of the box, Ma. It's a trick side. It opens inward." He put his hand in his pocket and pulled out a small key. "See this? With this I open the trick side from the inside. Then I pull the trick side down and crawl out between the ropes. Then I pull the side up again so no one can tell how I got in and out."

"Hmmmm." Mama thought about it. "You do it well, boys, very well."

But even with the new stunt, the brothers couldn't get work.

"Don't worry, Theo. Something'll happen. You'll see," Harry told his younger brother.

The younger boy looked at the older, wonder in his eyes. "You're always full of hope, Harry. I wish I could be like you."

A few days later they were hurrying home from another day of job hunting. There was still a little time before supper and Harry was eager to try out a new magic trick. They had just come in, and Harry had kissed his mother as he always did.

There was a knock on the door. Theo opened it. A tall, thin stranger stood there.

"You the Houdini Brothers?" he asked.

"Yes, that's us."

"They need you at the Imperial tonight." He explained that he was from the booking agent they had seen early that morning. "The opening act can't come. Got sick or something. Can you fellows make it?"

At last! A job in a real theater, they said to themselves.

"Thanks, mister." Harry was now at the door. "We'll be there." His voice was cool, calm.

When the man was gone, Harry burst out with excitement. "Our first break, Theo! Our first big break! This trick box did it. We're on our way!"

The young magicians arrived at the Imperial Theater long before show time. Harry walked up and down the empty aisles. A real theater! A real theater! he kept repeating to himself. He imagined the rows of seats filled with people eagerly waiting for him to appear. He could hear their wild applause after the act as he bowed again and again.

"Harry. Time to get ready," Theo exclaimed from the stage. "We have to get ready. We're the first act on the program." The first act was usually a "dumb" or silent act performed while latecomers were arriving and getting seated.

In the dressing room, the boys put on their second-hand evening clothes — black pants and jacket, a white shirt with a stiff white front and a black bow tie. Harry looked at the worn edges of his jacket sleeves and frowned. But he did look professional, he thought, as he glanced in the mirror. And he could do the tricks perfectly. He and Theo had practiced the box escape until they could change places in exactly three seconds. His frown melted into a confident smile.

There weren't many people in the audience for the early show. There rarely were. But the two boys performed as if the theater were full. They did their card and silk tricks. The audience applauded, but not loud enough for Harry.

It was time for the mystery box escape. Harry had decided to give the trick a new name — "Metamorphosis." "It's a fancy word for change," he had explained to his younger brother as they were going to the theater.

"Wait till they see Metamorphosis," Harry whispered to Theo as they waited for the box to be brought out.

Ra-ta-ta-ta! Drumbeats, then lively music. Harry walked to the center of the stage, and Theo followed. This was the biggest moment of Harry's life.

"Ladies and Gentlemen: With your kind permission, my brother Theo and I will now perform the great box escape. You will see the greatest mystery act in the world. My brother will get out of the box and I will get into the box without opening it," he announced, his eyes beaming with excitement.

The audience leaned forward and watched with interest as Theo was tied up, then placed in the sack, and finally locked into the box. Harry pulled the curtain closed and turned to the audience:

"When I clap my hands three times, behold a

miracle!" He clapped, then dashed behind the curtain, expecting Theo to dash in front of it. But something had gone wrong. Harry could hear his brother still in the box, struggling to get out. Quickly, he opened the box, and Theo climbed out, breathing hard. He had forgotten to take the small key that unlocked the box from the inside!

The audience booed!

After that catastrophe, the Houdini Brothers were unable to find any work. New York theaters didn't want young, inexperienced magicians without skill or talent.

"New York's not the only place on earth, Theo. There's a whole country, a whole world!" Harry Houdini declared to his brother, spreading his arms wide.

4

It'll Be a Great Life, Bess

After Theo had spoiled the Metamorphosis trick, the Houdini Brothers were unable to get work in New York. They couldn't even find work at neighborhood club meetings or parties. At that time, a great business depression was forcing factories and stores out of business. As a result, many people lost their jobs. In Harry's neighborhood many people were unemployed and had no money for entertainment. Some people did not even have enough money for food. So, Harry and Theo decided to go west to the Chicago World's Fair.

In 1893 the country was still celebrating the 400th anniversary of the discovery of America in 1492. The Fair had been planned for 1892, but it was a year late in opening.

"It's the biggest show on earth, Theo. The biggest," Harry repeated. "There'll be plenty of room for us there." His voice was filled with certainty. "We'll make a fortune in Chicago."

Rabbi Weiss had died earlier that year. It was important for Harry to earn money to contribute to the support of his mother and the younger children. He had promised his father. The two older brothers, Nathan and William, were working and contributing their share, too.

Taking with them their magic tricks and mystery box, the boys took a train to the Fair. Along the way, they stopped to give shows to earn money. When they reached the entertainment grounds in Chicago, Harry stared in amazement. There was so much going on — dancers, sword swallowers, trapeze artists, jugglers, fire eaters, and everything at the same time!

Crowds of people were everywhere. "Thousands will see us here, Theo," Harry said joyfully.

The young magicians found a job in a side show. Sometimes they did 20 shows a day, performing many kinds of tricks. Harry made a long line of silk handkerchiefs out of one hankerchief. He then made the line disappear. He caused a flower to appear after he touched a button-hole of his jacket with his wand. He made a pack of cards stand upright on the back of his hand. Theo performed coin tricks. They always closed with Metamorphosis. The mystery box escape always received the greatest applause.

Between shows, Harry watched the other magicians. He saw one trick that he never forgot. An East Indian magician swallowed a package of needles and a piece of thread. When he pulled the thread out of his mouth, all the needles were hanging on the thread in a straight line! He'd have to figure out how to do that one, he told himself.

Nothing up his sleeve!

When the job was over, the boys returned to New York. They found occasional work in beer halls and dime museums. In those days some museums were like circuses except that they did not have animal acts. Beer halls were noisy, crowded places where people often got drunk and poked fun at the performers. Harry couldn't stand being made fun of. He hated the beer halls.

In Huber's 14th Street Museum, Harry and Theo worked in a basement booth for a combined salary of $12.00 a week. The manager of the museum, a Mr. Anderson, had a hobby — escaping from ropes and handcuffs. He took a liking to Harry and offered to teach him these escapes. Harry was always eager to learn.

When payday came, he immediately bought a pair of handcuffs.

Each morning, Harry practiced the lessons he had learned the night before. Theo tied him with ropes and locked his hands in handcuffs. Harry found ways to free himself. But most museums and circuses were not yet interested in handcuff escapes. Only occasionally would the owner of a show permit handcuffs to be used.

When summer came, the brothers decided to go to Coney Island. At that time, Coney Island was a popular seashore resort. It was about an hour away by trolley from Manhattan. In the summertime, tens of thousands of people went there to swim. They also went there to enjoy the sideshows on a narrow street called the Bowery. The shows were similar to those at the Chicago World's Fair. Harry and Theo soon found work in one of the sideshows.

One night Harry met a young woman with pigtails. He was 19, she 18. He was Jewish. She was Catholic. She was doing a song and dance act with her sister under the stage name of Beatrice Raymond. Her real name was Wilhelmina Rahner. Harry fell in love with her and called her Bess.

A few weeks after they met they were married. They had three marriage ceremonies. First, a clerk married them at City Hall. Then, to please Bess's Catholic mother, a priest performed a ceremony. Finally, to satisfy Harry's Jewish mother, another ceremony was performed by a rabbi.

Harry had two birthdays and two names, and now he was married three times.

"It'll be a great life for us, Bess darling," he promised his pretty wife as they walked along the beach in the morning mist. "We'll be rich and famous. Everyone will know us!"

Bess looked at her young husband. How sure of himself, how determined he is, she thought. "I

Bess Houdini.

know they will, Harry," she answered, and she put her arm through his.

Theo left the act and started one of his own. Bess took his place, and the "Houdini Brothers" became the "Houdinis". The box trick became the most popular part of the act. Only now it was the trunk trick. Harry had bought a trunk for carrying their belongings, but he soon realized that it would be perfect for the escape trick. Harry and Bess practiced the trunk escape until they were able to do it in three seconds.

In the act, Bess wore pink tights and a glittering blouse; Harry wore a second-hand tuxedo. The first half of the act was made up of card and silk tricks, with Bess assisting Harry. Then they performed the trunk trick. When they finished, they would hold hands and take many deep bows to thank the audience for its applause.

When the summer was over, the young couple went back to Manhattan to work. Sometimes they found a job in a cheap theater, and they lived in a shabby room above it as part of their pay. When the job was over, they lived with Harry's family in the three room apartment on 69th Street. Sometimes, they traveled from town to town, together receiving a salary of $10 a week. Between jobs they had little to eat — maybe coffee and bread for breakfast, cheese and bread for supper.

Once Harry brought home a lonely puppy he had found in an alley. They shared what little they had with the hungry animal. Harry had nothing to send to his mother. This troubled him greatly. But he wrote to her every day.

The Houdinis were in a town in Virginia. They had just completed their act. Exhausted, Bess sat coughing in their drafty room. Harry felt miserable. He had promised Bess so much and had given her so little. If only something would happen, something good.

It did. One gloomy morning a telegram arrived from an agent offering them a job for a week at Tony Pastor's Theater. Pastor's, on 14th Street, was one of the great vaudeville theaters in New York. Vaudeville was a variety show of singers, dancers, comics, acrobats — entertainers of all kinds. Pastor's presented fine shows and had a well-dressed, well-educated audience. Harry's spirits were lifted until he counted his and Bess's money and found that they didn't have enough for the railroad fare north.

But the theater manager where they were appearing came to the rescue with a loan. And the Houdinis were able to leave for New York.

Upon arriving at Pastor's, a poster in the lobby informed them that there were sixteen acts in the show. Their act was the sixteenth. It was a great blow to Harry's pride. He thought a great deal of himself and of his ability. He believed he deserved a better spot on the program. To be the last one! It was almost more than he could bear. Bess tried to comfort him. "We're in New York, Harry, in a well-known theater. We're very lucky to be working here," she told him hopefully.

When their turn finally came, Harry, dressed in his second-hand tuxedo, performed his sleight of hand tricks. Bess, looking attractive in her colorful tights and glittering blouse, acted as his assistant.

Harry rolled up his sleeves. "Look carefully, ladies and gentlemen," he called out to the audience. "Nothing there." He flashed his winning smile. Then, with Bess handing him his equipment, he did his card and silk tricks, pulled a rabbit out of a silk hat, took an egg from an empty felt bag, and made a pigeon appear from nowhere. Then they both performed Metamorphosis — the mystery box escape.

The audience applauded wildly. As Harry took bow after bow, he felt that he was the finest magician in the world. But when the week was over, the Houdinis were again without a job.

5

Escape from a Straitjacket

The Welsh Brothers Traveling Circus in Philadelphia needed a magic act, and the Houdinis applied for the job. The job was for twenty weeks at $25.00 a week for both of them, plus food and room. They would travel in an old freight car and perform in a tent. It certainly was not Pastor's, but it would be steady work. Now Harry would be able to send money to Mama.

The circus had acrobats, a comic, a song and dance man, and many other acts. Harry's magic act was always popular and left the audience wondering. He had learned to use his hands and arms quickly and cleverly. This is an important skill for a magician because it keeps the audience's attention fixed on one spot. The magician then does the trick somewhere else. The audience sees only what the magician wants it to see.

After the mystery box escape, Bess did a singing clown number that the audience enjoyed.

"We need a wild man in a hurry, Houdini. Think you can do it?" the manager asked one afternoon. Harry could hear the crowd in front yelling to see the "Ferocious Wild Man" that the Welsh Brothers had advertised. In his contract, he had promised to help wherever he was needed.

With paint on his face, a costume made of gunnysack and his long bushy hair tangled around his face, Harry became the wild man. He sat in a cage growling and tearing at a piece of raw meat.

"In captivity this wild creature will eat nothing but raw meat and cigars," the ringmaster announced. People began to throw cigars at Harry, who never smoked. The "wild man" put on a good act of chewing and swallowing, while actually dropping the cigars into the gunnysack costume. The audience roared with laughter. Wild man Harry was a success. But he felt foolish.

At the end of each week Harry sent half of their $25 salary to his mother.

The Welsh Brothers circus traveled north, stopping to give shows along the way. One Sunday, they set up their tents and gave a show in Providence, Rhode Island. A state law there made it illegal to do shows on Sunday. After their performance, the entire troupe was arrested. They were put into small cells. They complained bitterly about

41

the arrests and their crowded cells. Harry felt disgraced and ashamed. A rabbi's son in prison. They stayed in jail until the following day, when John Welsh returned from New York and paid their fines.

When the circus closed, Harry and Bess teamed up with a magician who was going to Canada. They opened their show in Nova Scotia. But business was bad and the show closed.

Harry was beginning to understand that what he needed was publicity to get people to come to the theater. "I have to get our name in the newspapers, Bess" he insisted. "People must read about us and talk about us." Bess agreed.

He thought up a stunt. He would escape from ropes that tied him to a horse running through the streets. To be sure of publicity, he got the owner of a local newspaper and other important people in the town to come out to watch him.

Harry was tied to the back of a horse he had rented from a local stable. His hands were tied behind him. His feet were tied underneath the horse's belly.

Harry had made sure to ask the stable keeper for a tame horse. But much to his surprise, before the last knot was tied, the horse began to race wildly through the town. Harry couldn't stop it. He would be killed if he tried to escape. He was terrified. Finally, exhausted, the horse stopped in an empty field, far from the waiting group. Having learned how to escape from ropes, Harry untied himself and walked back to town, embarrassed. He had learned a lesson — never to do anything in public that he hadn't tried before.

Determined to make a success in Canada, Harry and Bess left Nova Scotia and moved on to New Brunswick. Here Harry met a doctor who took him to visit a hospital for the mentally ill, where violent patients were often put into straitjackets to restrain them. Harry watched with pity as a patient in a padded cell struggled to free himself from the heavy canvas jacket. The jacket had a leather collar. Its sleeves were very long and sewn at the ends. A leather strap was attached at the end of each sleeve. The jacket opened in the back. "It's impossible to escape from one of those," the doctor remarked.

Impossible. The very word was a challenge to Harry Houdini. He thought about it all night. "I can do it, Bess. I can do it," he told her the next morning. The doctor loaned him a straitjacket, and Harry began to practice his escape.

With Bess's help, he pushed his hands into the long sleeves. Bess strapped and buckled him up in the back. Harry crossed his arms over his chest. The extremely long sleeves met in the back and

43

Harry being strapped into a straitjacket.

Bess strapped and buckled them together. With his hands fastened firmly behind his back, it seemed a person could not possibly get out of a straitjacket.

Harry's big problem was to get his arms in front. Then he would be able to open the straps and buckles. Harry had figured out how to do it during the night.

Now he placed an elbow on the dresser in his

room. By great strength and effort, he forced his arms over his head and in front of him. He used his teeth to open the buckles and straps that fastened the sleeves together. Now he had to reach the buckles and straps behind him. Although his strong fingers were still stuck in the sewn up sleeves, he moved them through the heavy canvas to the back of the jacket and freed himself. It was a difficult but very satisfying stunt.

Every night and early morning, Harry practiced getting out of the jacket. When he could do the escape perfectly, he would be ready to perform it on stage.

In the theater he invited a member of the audience to strap him into the jacket. Then he went inside his cabinet. The curtain was closed. A few minutes later Harry appeared before the audience, sweating, exhausted, free. To his great surprise, there was hardly a handclap. For the simple trunk escape, audiences went wild. For this difficult escape, there was silence. He was puzzled.

Penniless, Bess and Harry boarded a ship for home. They had persuaded the captain to let them entertain the passengers in return for their passage. But Harry became seasick, too sick to do anything but lie in his bunk. Fortunately, some kind passengers contributed money to pay for Bess's food.

6

Escape from Handcuffs

"Bess, I'm through with show business. I'm 24 and I've gotten nowhere."

They were sitting on a bed that served as a sofa in the living room on East 69th Street. Harry's head was bowed between his hands. "We don't even have a home of our own. It's just been a struggle for you, Bess."

Bess put her arms around her husband. It hurt her to see him feeling so low. "It's no struggle if it's with you, Harry," she said softly. "Some day we'll have everything we want."

Harry was too depressed to be cheered. He had no job, nor any clues about where to find one. He felt as if the theaters of the world would be closed to him forever. He would have to find another way to earn a living in the magic field, he thought. So, with a loan from his brother, Nathan, he opened a school for magic. When that failed, he tried selling magic equipment. He even offered to sell some of his secrets to newspaper owners. But no one would buy them — not even at the bargain price of $20.

"Harry, my sister's husband says he can get you a job with the manufacturer of Yale locks," Bess said after a visit to one of her sisters. For a moment his eyes brightened. He might consider a job like that. He sat deep in thought. Then he arose and left the house. He could always think better while walking.

One evening after dinner Harry and Bess sat talking about their problems.

"My life is in show business, Bess," he told her. "There's no other way for me." Bess nodded. "I know," she answered.

The Houdinis continued to look for work. They found jobs for a few days, sometimes a week. One jobless day, Harry stole a handful of potatoes to keep them from starving.

After several months, they found a steady job with an old-fashioned traveling medicine show. At these shows, bottles of "medicine" were sold by a fake doctor wearing a white coat. He promised that what was inside the bottle could cure boils, colds, rheumatism, everything, even deafness.

The show was booked to play in Kansas. The Houdinis took a train to get there. On the way they had to make a quick change of trains in the middle of the night. There were no porters around to transfer their luggage from one train to the other. Harry had managed some of it himself. But two trunks containing their stage equipment were still in the first train when he heard the conductor say "All aboard as is going aboard." Harry begged the conductor to wait until he could get the two trunks. Their act could not go on without the equipment, he explained.

"Can't do that, young fellow. Have to follow the time schedule," the conductor answered sharply.

The Houdinis spent a lot of time waiting in train stations.

The whistle blew. The train began to move. Harry jumped down, ran ahead of the train and flung himself on the tracks. Brakes screeched. The train stopped. The angry conductor yelled for Harry to get up, but Harry refused to move until his trunks were taken aboard.

Finally in Kansas, the Houdinis and the traveling medicine show stopped and set up their tent wherever the owners thought business would be good.

After "Dr." Hill or "Dr." Pratt, who were the owners of the show spoke to the audience about their medicine, Harry and Bess entertained. During the entertainment the two fake doctors went among the audience to sell their bottles of fake medicine. Sometimes Bess helped the men sell while Harry performed his magic and escape tricks.

Harry's equipment now included many pairs of handcuffs. Ever since he had bought his first pair, he had been fascinated by them. He read every book he could find on the subject. In every city in which they stopped, he went to pawnshops and bought handcuffs of different makes. He visited locksmith shops to learn more about locks. He knew from his job in the locksmith's shop when he was nine that many locks and cuffs could be opened with the same key, or with a lockpick.

Now he decided to add a handcuff trick to the act. But first he practiced a lot. He discovered that he could open some handcuffs just by striking the cuffs against a piece of metal that was tied to his knee under his trousers. He also found that he could open the cuffs by holding a key between his teeth. Finally, he could open either cuff with the opposite hand. He had practiced doing things with both hands so that now he could use one hand almost as easily as the other.

After Harry could do handcuff escapes perfectly, he made them a regular part of his act. But the applause for them was not great. He wondered what was wrong.

"I must figure it out, Bess," he said one night after a performance. He thought about it for several months before he found a solution. He had been opening the handcuffs in full view of the audience. They could see how easy it was for him. Now he would open them inside his cabinet, with only his face visible. The audience would see the strain and great pain he would pretend to be suffering as he struggled to free himself of the cuffs. This would add mystery and suspense to his act.

But he still needed a publicity stunt to bring the people to the theater.

While working in Chicago at Kohl and Middleton's Museum, Harry became friendly with some newspaper reporters. They were good for publicity and they knew many people. Harry got one of them to introduce him to the chief of detectives, Lieutenant Rohan. A day or two later he went with Bess to visit Rohan at the city jail. Rohan was charmed by Houdini's wife and the stories she told about their adventures in show business. As she spoke to Rohan, Harry sneaked into the jail and took a quick but careful look at the locks on the cell doors. In a few minutes, he was back beside Bess, saying goodbye to the unsuspecting Rohan.

"You did a good job talking to the Lieutenant, sweetheart," he said when they were safely on the street.

"Did you learn what you wanted, Harry?"

"You bet I did. I remember every lock in that jail."

The next day he invited several newspaper reporters and a news photographer to go with him to the city jail. "You'll get a great story," he promised. Rohan was in his office when they arrived.

"I challenge you to handcuff me and lock me in a cell. Then I'll escape from that cell," Harry announced. Rohan wasn't against a little publicity, especially if he could make a young smart aleck look like a fool. As the reporters watched, Rohan placed three pairs of handcuffs on Harry's wrists. Then he locked him in a cell. The reporters and

51

Rohan all went into Rohan's office and sat down. Rohan took a pack of cards from his desk. "He'll be there a long time," he said, turning his head in the direction of the cells. But before he could finish dealing, Harry walked into the office. Harry

A publicity picture of a jail escape.

had expected to be met with surprise and admiration. Instead he was faced by reporters who felt they had been cheated.

"What have you got on you — a set of keys? Rohan tells us you were here yesterday," one of the reporters called out.

"Search me and see," Harry answered.

Even after a newsman searched him and found nothing, the reporters were still doubtful. To make sure he had not slipped a key into a hidden pocket Harry was made to undress. He was then handcuffed and locked in a cell. His clothes were locked in another cell. In a few minutes Harry again stood in Rohan's office, dressed and smiling. The news photographers clicked their cameras.

That was just what Harry had wanted — publicity. The next day when his picture appeared in the newspaper, he bought every copy he could find and sent the story of his cell escape to agents in New York. "Wait till those agents see this," he said as he and Bess walked to the mailbox. But not one agent wrote back to him. However, the publicity brought more people to see him wherever they stopped.

In every town, Harry went with the newspaper reporters to the jail and challenged the police to handcuff him and lock him in their strongest cell. He always escaped.

"We're lucky this guy is not a criminal, or we'd sure have trouble on our hands," said the police chief of one town, laughing.

Harry Houdini had invented a new kind of magic — the magic of escape. He was always thinking how to make his escapes dramatic, and exciting. Now he added a new element to his act — the challenge!

Harry generally lay in bed at night thinking up new stunts or ways of improving old ones. After his usual five hours of sleep, he awoke early and entered notes in his notebook about his new ideas. He tried them out to see if they could be done, and then practiced for months. By the time Bess awoke, he usually had a cup of fresh coffee ready for her and an idea to discuss with her.

"Bess, I've found a way to make the handcuff escapes really exciting." He didn't wait for her to ask how. "I'm going to challenge the public to bring their own handcuffs to the theater for me to open."

He ordered handbills printed to advertise the challenge and passed them out on the street.

One evening he stood before an audience in a theater in St. Paul, Minnesota. "Ladies and Gentlemen: I challenge anyone to keep me locked in any regulation handcuffs that he or she has brought. Whoever has cuffs is invited to come up here and put me to the test. I promise to break free." He then invited other volunteers to come to the stage to see that everything was done honestly.

After the handcuffs were locked on him, Harry stepped inside his cabinet. The orchestra played fast, exciting music. The people waited. In less than a minute he stepped out and dropped the handcuffs onto the stage where they landed with a clatter. He bowed to an admiring and applauding audience.

One night after a performance, a stranger stopped the Houdinis as they left the theater. "Will you and Mrs. Houdini have supper with me?" he asked Harry. Harry gladly accepted. Such invitations were rare.

"That's a good act you have," the stranger said when they were seated. "But it could be better." Harry didn't like criticism, and sometimes he got angry quickly. But he was also curious. The man was well dressed and he seemed to know about show business.

"What's wrong with the act?" Harry asked sharply.

"There's too much in it. It's too crowded," the stranger explained. "If you'd leave out the magic — just stick to the trunk and handcuff escapes, especially that challenge to the audience — you could work in my theaters."

Work in his theaters? Harry thought excitedly, as his manner quickly softened.

"What's your name, sir?"

"Martin Beck. I hire talent for the Orpheum Circuit."

Harry could barely hide his joy. The Orpheum Circuit was a chain of vaudeville theaters located in large cities in the Midwest and West. Martin Beck could be an important person in his life.

Mr. Beck offered the Houdinis sixty dollars a week to start. They would meet the next day to discuss the details.

Harry and Bess left the restaurant happier than they had been in a long time.

"This is the best opportunity we've ever had, Bess." "And the best salary we've ever made!" answered Bess. "Imagine! Sixty dollars a week! We'll be rich in no time."

"And famous, too," Harry was quick to add.

The next morning they met with Martin Beck to find out where they were going. The first stop would be San Francisco. Then they would do shows in Orpheum Theaters in Omaha, St. Louis, Kansas City, Memphis, Nashville, and Los Angeles.

As they traveled, Harry tried to learn ahead of time the locks used by the police in the next city on their tour. If he got this information he would twist a piece of wire to fit the lock. Sometimes, such a pick could open both the cell door and the corridor door of the same jail. If he couldn't find out, he found other ways. Upon arrival, he would get permission from the police to walk through the jail and look at the locks. With a tiny piece of special wax in the palm of his hand, he would press up against a lock and take an impression of it. Then he would either have a key made or make a lockpick. Harry was using the same tools and methods used by all magicians, but he was using them with more skill and daring.

In Omaha, he escaped from leg irons and five pairs of handcuffs. In San Francisco he got out of irons on his arms and legs, and a chain of handcuffs connecting the arm and leg irons. He could barely move on his own and had to be carried to the cell. Ten minutes after the cell had been locked he was free!

In some jails, he was examined thoroughly by a doctor while naked. No one ever found a key or a pick on him. They didn't know where to look. He hid a small pick or key in his nose, or ears, or he glued it to the sole of his foot. On stage, he hid his keys under the carpet or in the curtains of the cabinet.

In some shows, he escaped after being tied to a chair with a long rope. While being bound, he would expand his body by swelling his chest and

stretching his arms. After he relaxed his body, he had enough distance between himself and the rope to undo the knots that were holding him to the chair. He preferred being tied with a thick new rope because its knots were easier to undo. He opened the knots with his hands, his toes or his teeth.

Newspapers printed stories of his prison escapes, and people came to the theater to see the Handcuff King. Audiences at Orpheum Theaters grew larger and larger. As a result, his salary of sixty dollars a week was increased steadily until it reached one hundred and twenty-five dollars a week. That was a huge sum of money in 1899.

Harry was happy. Now he had more money to send to his mother, and he could buy many books. Books were important to him. He had inherited his father's love for learning. To Harry, however, learning meant mainly finding out everything there was to know about his profession.

After he finished practicing his stunts each day, he practiced his speech. Ever since a manager had corrected his English, he had been determined to improve it. He wanted every part of his performance to be perfect. Except for his five hours of sleep a night, the rest of his time he spent on his work.

In the fall of 1899, the Orpheum tour was over. Harry and Bess took the train to New York. They thought surely there would be bookings waiting for them in the East. But only a few calls came. The New York agents were not impressed with success in theaters in the Midwest and the West. Only Eastern theaters were important to them.

Harry was bitterly disappointed. But he no longer had any thoughts about leaving show business. He would have to find some way to get into the large eastern theaters.

7

Escape from Scotland Yard

Harry decided to go to Europe. If he was successful there, then America would want him. It had
happened to his friend, T. Nelson Downs, whom
he had met at the Chicago Fair. Downs' specialty
was coin tricks. He was now famous as the "King
of Koins." The same had happened to other magicians after successful performances in Europe.

"But you don't know anyone in Europe," Bess
protested. "What will you do there?"

"I'll find a way, Bess. I'm sure I will."

"I guess we can always go back to the dime museums," Bess sighed.

"Never, Bess. Never!"

They began to plan for the trip. On May 30,
1900, the day of departure, his mother, sister,
brothers, cousins, aunts and uncles went with
Harry and Bess to the dock.

"When will you be back, my son?" Mrs. Weiss
asked Harry as she hugged him.

61

"I don't know," he answered weakly. Harry held on to his mother.

A few hours later he was lying in his bunk seasick, wishing that boats had never been invented. He was sick during the entire trip.

After their arrival in London, Harry went to see booking agents. One of the agents, Harry Day, a man of about Harry's age, was impressed with Harry's confidence and determination.

"I'll introduce you to Mr. Slater, the manager of the Alhambra," Day offered. "It's one of the best theaters in London."

The next day they went by horse and buggy to Slater's office. When Harry told Slater that he could escape from any handcuffs, Mr. Slater took him to Scotland Yard, the headquarters of the British police force. Scotland Yard was known all over the world for its brilliant work in finding criminals.

"So, you think you can escape from our handcuffs?" asked the Scotland Yard superintendent, dangling a pair of shiny cuffs in front of Harry. Harry looked at the cuffs carefully. He had learned that English cuffs were easier to open than American cuffs. They were the kind that could be opened by being hit against something hard.

"Yes, sir," he answered confidently.

On board ship with Charlie and a young fellow-passenger.

"Then put your arms around this," the superintendent ordered, pointing to a strong post in his office. Harry did as he was told. "Here's how we fasten Yankee criminals who come here to get into trouble, the superintendent said with a laugh."

He and Slater turned to leave the room. But before they got to the door, Harry rapped the cuffs against the post. Just as he had figured, they fell to the floor and made a loud noise.

"This is the way Yankees get out of handcuffs," Harry said, with victory in his voice.

Two weeks later, the King of Handcuffs stood on the brightly lit stage of the Alhambra Theater. His first performance in Europe! He felt that a new life was beginning for him.

"Ladies and Gentlemen," he greeted his European audience with his warm smile. "With your permission I shall challenge anyone in this theater . . ." Before he could finish, a man ran onto the stage shouting that he, Cirnoc, was the King of Handcuffs. "You're a fake, Houdini, not even an American. You've never even been in America."

Harry was too stunned to answer.

Suddenly a man's voice came from the audience. "I have seen and heard Mr. Houdini perform in the United States. I know that he is an American." It was the voice of Chauncey Depew, a famous

American lawyer and businessman. Houdini was grateful to this friend whom he had never met.

Houdini always carried with him a large collection of handcuffs. Now he whispered to Bess. She went behind the curtain and returned with a pair of giant cuffs.

"I'll give you five hundred dollars if you can escape from these, Cirnoc."

"Let's see if *you* can do it first," Cirnoc replied.

Harry stretched out his arms. Cirnoc snapped the cuffs on him. Harry stepped into his cabinet. In a moment he stepped out, offering the cuffs to his challenger. Now Cirnoc had to accept.

Harry snapped the cuffs on him. Then he surprised everyone by giving Cirnoc the key to the handcuffs. Cirnoc went into the cabinet. Minutes passed. The audience began to laugh. Finally, red in the face and angry, Cirnoc came out, his hands still locked in the cuffs. He had been unable to reach the keyhole of the cuffs. While the audience applauded and Houdini bowed, Cirnoc rushed off the stage.

For publicity for the show, Harry hired men to walk through the busy streets of London wearing sandwich boards with HOUDINI — ALHAMBRA in large letters. His opinion of himself was so great that he expected everyone to recognize his name at once. He gave theater passes to newspaper reporters. Most of them wrote articles of praise. But if a reporter wrote an article against him, Harry became unhappy. He wanted praise from everyone.

Soon people stood in long lines to buy tickets. When Houdini's two week stay was up, Slater asked him to stay two more weeks. Then two more. Soon Houdini became known throughout England and Europe. Harry Day, who was now his agent, booked him into the Central Theater in Dresden, Germany.

In Dresden, Harry found that German handcuffs were stronger and heavier and more difficult to open than American or English cuffs. He spent many hours each day in locksmith shops learning all he could about German locks and cuffs. He bought several of each and took them apart to learn how they were made.

On his first night at the Central Theater, the manager warned him, "If the audience whistles, your job here is over." Whistling in Germany meant the same as booing in the United States. Harry was worried. The first difficulty he had to meet was making an opening speech in German. Fortunately he remembered some of the German he had heard his parents speak all through his childhood. Now he 'stood before the audience, searching for the right words, stumbling over some, smiling in apology when he used the wrong word. But when he finished the audience burst into applause. He had spoken to the people in their language, and they liked it. He felt closer to them and they to him. What did it matter that he made errors? His enthusiasm was great. The audience caught his spirit and forgave his mistakes.

After his speech, Harry performed his challenge and handcuff escapes, then he did the mystery box escape with Bess. When the act was over, the audience stood and cheered. Harry sighed with relief. His audience was not whistling, but cheering.

Houdini was still challenging the police in each city to handcuff him and lock him into their most secure cell. But now he wanted something new — a more daring publicity stunt. He wanted to attract the same large audiences he had enjoyed in England. He would have to think of something exciting.

Harry's creative mind could find ideas anywhere — in a mental hospital, a prison, on a river, a bridge. One sunny morning as he stood on a bridge looking down upon the Elbe River, an idea came to him. The Elbe is one of the important rivers in Germany. Large boats carrying freight to and from many ports pass 'through it. As Harry watched the flow of the river, the idea took shape. He would jump into the river, his hands and feet bound in irons. It would be a great publicity stunt.

Houdini was an excellent swimmer, a high diver and a strong under-water swimmer. He had learned water sports during his days with the Pastime Athletic Club. Since that time he had kept himself in good physical condition by running. Now he swam

Getting ready for a jump into the river.

daily, too. He practiced holding his breath under water until he was able to perform the stunt with complete safety.

Finally, with hundreds of people watching, Harry leaped from a bridge, his hands locked in cuffs, his feet in chains. Yet in a few minutes he rose to the surface, hands and feet free. The crowds cheered.

After that performance great crowds came to the theater to see him. His popularity in Germany grew. The manager in Dresden wanted him to come back. A theater in Berlin was asking for him. Slater wanted him back in London.

"Maybe there should be two of me," he said to Bess. "I can hardly keep up with one of you," she laughed.

There were days when Houdini did not take time to eat. Once before a show, Bess prepared a mixture of two quarts of milk and a dozen eggs. Harry swallowed it all in the dressing room.

"I'd starve without you, sweetheart," he said, leaning over to kiss her.

"I'd never let you, Harry," she answered, returning his kiss as she straightened his bow tie.

Bess now appeared on stage only when they performed the mystery trunk escape. She took care of Harry's wardrobe, managed his money, and helped settle arguments with his assistants. Harry now had two assistants as well as a skilled mechanic who made his equipment in Harry's own workshop.

With requests to perform in Dresden, Berlin, and London, Harry asked his brother Theo to come to Europe. Theo was working in the United States as a magician under the name of Hardeen. Harry cabled him: "There's work here for both of us. Come as soon as you can." Theo came. He already knew some of Harry's stunts. Harry taught him others and gave him equipment. He was not afraid of competition from his brother. He knew that he was better than Theo. While Harry worked in one city, Theo worked in another. They came together as often as they could to discuss their work and talk about the family. Theo told him that his brother Leopold had become a doctor. Harry was proud of Leopold and glad he had become a success.

The Houdinis loved children. But, to their sorrow, they had none. Instead they occupied themselves with pets — cats, dogs, birds, and guinea pigs. When their dog, Charlie, died, Harry cried. They soon got a new terrier, Bobby. Harry had tiny handcuffs and a straitjacket made for Bobby and trained him to escape. "You're training a com-

Escaping from the straitjacket. →

petitor," Bess warned him. They both had a good laugh.

Harry found out that Theo was performing the straitjacket escape in full view of the audience and receiving tremendous applause. Harry was still doing it inside the curtained cabinet. He had wondered why this difficult stunt was not popular with his audiences.

"It's because the people can't see you," Theo explained. "They think that someone is helping you inside that cabinet."

"You're right, Theo." Harry didn't like to admit that his younger brother had worked out the stunt better than he. He wished he had realized his mistake himself.

When Harry performed the straitjacket escape

the next time, he lay on the stage, rolling and twisting to get free of the garment. The audience could see the struggle, the strain, and the sweat. Now instead of a few handclaps, there was shouting and wild applause. Harry liked nothing better than applause.

In December of 1900, Houdini returned to London to perform again at the Alhambra. A month later, while walking by a London store, Harry saw a dress in the window. A small sign read "designed for the Queen." England's Queen Victoria had died a few days before. As Harry looked at the dress, he thought of his mother. She was about the same size as the queen. Why not buy it for Mama? he thought.

He went into the shop, but the owner was not eager to sell. Harry finally bought the dress, but only after promising that it would not be worn in England.

Harry had written his mother every day since he had left the United States. Now he asked her to come to Europe. "I have a surprise for you when you arrive, Mama," he wrote. In the envelope he enclosed a check for the trip.

When Cecilia Weiss arrived, Houdini was in Germany performing in a theater in Hamburg. She went with him to the theater that night. "There isn't an empty seat in the house," the manager told him.

"Then make one," Harry ordered. "It's for my mother."

A chair was brought from one of the dressing rooms and placed in an area reserved for special guests. Mrs. Weiss watched with pleasure as her son performed before a cheering crowd.

On the way to an appearance in Germany.

Harry still spoke with his mother in Yiddish. He told her about the surprise he had for her — a visit to Budapest to see her family. Tears came to Mrs. Weiss's eyes. It was twenty-seven years since she had left Hungary to make her home in the United States. When the show was over, Bess, Harry, and his mother boarded a train for Budapest. Harry had made arrangements for a big party at the Royal Hotel where his mother was to stay.

Dressed in a queen's gown, Cecilia Weiss sat as proudly as a queen in the Royal Hotel's Palm Gardens. Her son stood beside her. Their eyes glowed with happiness as relatives and friends came to greet them.

A few days later, Mrs. Weiss returned home. Bess and Harry continued to travel throughout Europe. There were still places to see, new audiences to entertain, and new stunts to perform. His next performance would be in Holland, where he would perform with a famous circus.

But his goal was still New York — to work in the fine theaters there. Only then would he feel fully successful.

8

A New Home

A day before the circus opened, Bess and Harry were watching windmills turn in a lovely countryside in Holland. Bess saw excitement in Harry's eyes.

"I'm going to escape from a moving windmill, Bess!"

The next day Harry was tied with a rope to the arm of a large windmill. It began to turn. Before Harry could free himself, the arm of the windmill broke and Harry crashed to the ground. Fortunately, his only injuries were scratches and bruises. But his pride was hurt for he had failed in public.

Back in England, Harry introduced a stunt that he had learned years before at the Chicago World's Fair: the East Indian Needle Trick. He had practiced it many times until he had perfected the stunt. He placed a package of needles and a long piece of thread in his mouth. Then he took a drink of water. With the spotlight shining on him and the orchestra playing softly, he slowly pulled the thread from his mouth. The needles, threaded and hanging evenly, gleamed through the darkness of the theater. To great applause, Harry bowed deeply. He was very pleased with himself, for he

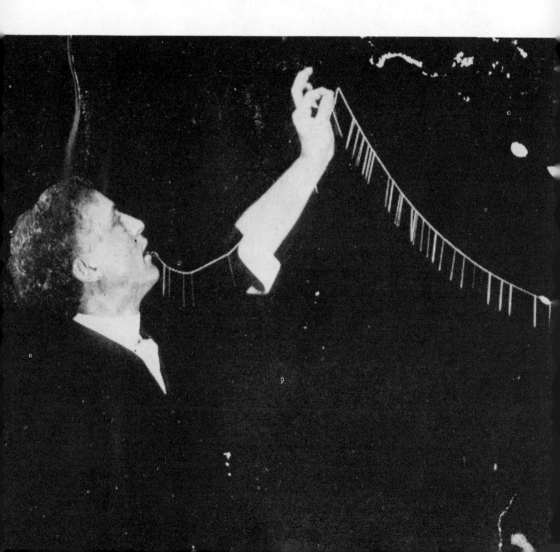

had learned to control the muscles of his throat. He could swallow an object and then bring it back up.

Harry performed a dramatic escape when several British sailors challenged him to stand in front of a loaded cannon that was set to go off in twenty minutes. Before an audience, Harry was tied to the muzzle of the cannon. His hands and feet were bound with rope. He had to act quickly — his opponent was time. He immediately kicked off his shoes and untied the knots with his bare toes. Then he twisted and turned his way out of the ropes that tied him to the cannon. He was free in seventeen minutes — only 3 minutes from blast-off time!

With each new trick, Harry's popularity rose. People stood in line for hours waiting to buy tickets to see his shows.

Houdini's next stop was Paris. He learned that Mrs. Robert-Houdin still lived there. She was the widow of the great magician whose life story had started young Ehrich Weiss on a career of magic. He wrote to her, asking to see her. She refused and accused him of stealing her husband's name. Harry was deeply hurt, and he never forgave her.

Harry had never performed in Russia. "It's a huge country and the people like theater," he told

Harry Day. So, his agent booked him for four weeks in a Moscow theater.

When they arrived in Russia, Harry had to give a speech in Russian. A friend helped him. Harry tried it out on the manager of the theater. The man frowned. "You're not talking Russian, Houdini," he said, "you're talking Polish with a Yiddish accent." Harry was grateful that he had not yet made the speech before an audience.

A Russian who understood English translated Harry's speech into Russian. Then he wrote it out in English letters. With paper in hand, Harry went to a Moscow park to practice the speech. As he stood under a tree, he raised his voice as if he were on a stage. A crowd gathered. They did not understand what Harry was doing. Not knowing Russian, Harry could not explain his actions. The police took him to the local jail. It required both Bess and the theater manager to convince the police that he was the famous magician who had come to Russia to entertain.

Harry's performance — the handcuff escapes, the East Indian needle trick, the mystery trunk escape — attracted such large audiences that the four-week stay was extended to twelve.

During their travels through Europe, Harry visited book shops, magic shops and antique shops.

He bought a great number of magic articles, including equipment used by famous magicians who had died. He bought books, programs, photos, and many other items having to do with magic.

Bess looked at the huge collection that increased every day. "Where will we keep it?" she asked with doubt in her voice.

"We'll find a place," he assured her. Every piece was precious to him. "I think it's time we had a home, sweetheart, a large one." They had been living in rooming houses and hotels for almost ten years.

Bess looked at Harry and smiled. "Yes, it is, Harry," she said softly. That was her dream, too.

But as a result of constant travel and work, Houdini became ill. The doctor was called and he ordered rest. Harry obeyed orders for a week. Then he and Bess went to New York.

Harry spent the spring of 1904 resting and visiting with his mother, who still lived in the tenement on East 69th Street. He also looked for a house that would be suitable for Bess, his mother, and his huge collection of books and magical things.

"I have a surprise for you, Ma," he told her one evening.

Mrs. Weiss laughed. "Another surprise?" She

An example of the huge crowds that Harry Houdini drew to his stunts.

remembered that wonderful visit to Budapest.

The next morning they took a cab uptown and stopped in front of a brownstone house on West 113th Street.

"Our new home, Mama. You've lived long enough on 69th Street."

Mrs. Weiss looked up at the four-story house. Then she followed Harry into the building. She walked through the twenty-six rooms, staring wide-eyed. "But what will we do with all of these rooms, Ehrich?" she asked several times.

"You'll see, Mama."

A few weeks later Mrs. Weiss looked in amazement as her son unpacked hundreds of handcuffs and keys, magic articles, and all the other things he had brought home from Europe. This included over five thousand books about theater, witchcraft, escapes, and magic. The huge book collection filled three rooms.

Harry made changes in the house. He built secret trap doors and sliding walls. Most importantly, he had a giant bathtub put into one of the rooms so that he could practice underwater stunts. That was to be his next big feature.

When his mother and Bess were comfortably settled, and Harry felt completely well, he went to see theater managers and agents. During his four years in Europe, he had sent them newspaper clippings of his successes. Still they were not impressed. He received a few job offers, but the salaries offered were an insult to him. In Europe he had earned over a thousand dollars a week. He felt hurt and angry.

"They don't appreciate me here, Bess. We're going back to Europe. They'll have to beg me to return."

In August of 1904 they returned to Europe.

One night after a show in London, Houdini entered his dressing room, makeup still on his face, applause still in his ears. Bess and Harry Day were inside waiting for him. Harry was surprised to see his agent. They had already spoken together that day.

"A cable arrived this afternoon, Harry" Day began. "There's a job for you in New York. It pays a thousand dollars a week."

Harry looked at Bess. "New York is finally waking up," he said as a smile moved across his face.

9

Watery Escapes

Back in the United States, Houdini played at the famous Colonial Theater in New York. Then, he went on a tour of several big cities. In Washington he performed a stunt that brought him publicity throughout the country. He escaped from a cell that once held the murderer of President James A. Garfield.

The cell had heavy bars across the door and a lock with five tumblers. Harry, with his hands and feet in irons, was locked in the cell. In exactly two minutes he was out. But before he returned to the warden's office where newspaper reporters were waiting for him, he unlocked all the cells in a row. He ordered the prisoners out and told them to take other cells. It made great publicity.

This was the beginning of a new publicity routine. In the summer he escaped from rivers. In the winter he escaped from jails. His name was in the headlines and his picture on the front page throughout the year.

As Harry's fame grew, other escapists imitated his stunts. They called themselves "handcuff kings". Because of the competition, his popularity fell. Now he saw many empty seats in theaters. He was angry and bitter. He didn't like the competition. He felt that the challenge handcuff act belonged to him and anyone else who used it was a thief. He challenged his competitors to escape from handcuffs that he would provide. He threatened to sue them. But nothing that he did stopped them. To win back his popularity, he would have to find new escapes and improve on old ones.

Between publicity stunts and shows, Houdini did other things having to do with magic. He became president of the Society of American Magicians. He helped organize magic clubs throughout the United States and then made them part of the society.

He wrote books on magic which explained how he did some of his tricks. Among these books were *Handcuff Secrets*, *Magical Rope Ties and Escapes*, and *Paper Magic*. He was not afraid to let his readers know some of his secrets because he was sure that he could perform his tricks better than anyone else. He also wrote a book called *The Right Way to do Wrong,* telling how some criminals committed their crimes. Harry also owned and directed a magazine for magic fans called *The Conjurors Monthly.* By writing about his knowledge and putting out a magazine, he felt he was continuing the family's scholarly tradition.

Between books, Harry tried new stunts. One day after escaping from a river, he thought, why not try a water escape on stage? He discussed the idea with Bess and his assistants. For many months Harry and his assistants worked on the stunt until they were certain of it.

On the night of January 27, 1908 in a theater in St. Louis, the lights dimmed. The curtains opened on an iron milk can about 42 inches high that was barely large enough for a man to squeeze into. The orchestra played a lively march. Harry, dressed in an elegant black tuxedo, walked to the center of the stage. The music stopped.

"Ladies and Gentlemen," his voice rang out. "My latest invention — The Milk Can. I will be placed in this can which soon will be filled with water. A committee from the audience will lock the padlocks and place the keys in front of the footlights. I will attempt to escape. Should I fail to appear within a certain time, my assistants will open the curtains, smash the can, and do everything possible to save my life. Music, maestro, please."

While his assistants were filling the can with water and the orchestra played, Houdini went into his dressing room and changed into a bathing suit.

A river jump . . .

Back on the stage, his hands and feet were locked in irons. He was lifted and placed in the can feet first. Water spilled over the top. The lid of the can was locked with six padlocks. Then a cabinet was placed over the can.

While the orchestra played *Asleep in the Deep*,

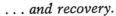

. . . and recovery.

people in the audience held their breath. Others began to count the minutes. One minute, two minutes — the minutes seemed like hours. An assistant with a fire axe came onto the stage, to enter the cabinet and break the can. He was not needed, however, as Harry suddenly appeared before the audience, smiling and dripping with water. The audience stopped counting, sighed with relief, and broke into great applause.

"That man must have supernatural power," some said as they left the theater.

But Houdini had often told his audiences that he had no supernatural powers. He had said that his stunts were the result of knowledge, skill and constant practice. He also gave credit to his strength. Through the years he had continued to exercise in order to keep himself physically fit.

If he had no supernatural powers, then how had he escaped from the milk can?

Houdini and his assistants had built the can in the basement workshop of his home. Its shape included sloping shoulders, for that was the shape of milk cans then. If a committee had come to examine the can, it would have found that the shoulders were fastened to the body of the can with rivets. But the rivets were fake — they were just dummy ends. All that Harry had to do was to push his head hard against the lid, and the entire upper part of the can came off.

News of the milk can stunt spread to Europe. Theater managers called for him. Harry traveled back and forth between Europe and the United States filling engagements.

Always searching for new challenges, Harry found one in Europe. While performing in Hamburg, Germany, in 1909, Houdini went to see an aviation exhibition. Very few people flew airplanes at that time. The first airplane flight had been made only six years before by the Wright Brothers. Harry watched as the airplane rose into the air, circled the field, and returned safely to the ground. Now it was he who gazed in wonder.

He must learn to fly this new vehicle, he thought. He was determined to own one, no matter what the cost.

Very shortly afterward, he bought a plane, painted his name in large letters on the side, and hired a pilot to teach him how to fly. After a number of lessons, he decided he was ready to go up by himself. One calm day he climbed into his precious plane, started the engine, and took off. But before he knew what had happened, he had crash landed. He was stunned, but not hurt. Only the aircraft was damaged. But Houdini was satisfied. He had been up for several seconds. When the machine was repaired, he tried again. This time he landed safely. He felt that he had conquered space!

When he went to Australia to perform, he took the plane with him. It was expensive, but he was eager to continue this new interest. Every day between shows he drove his new car to the flying field — he had also learned to drive — and practiced flying. One fine, clear day, he took off and stayed in the air for three minutes! Before he left Australia, he was presented with a plaque by the Aerial League of Australia for being the first successful aviator on that continent. Harry was pleased with himself.

When he left Australia, he gave up both flying and driving an automobile. He would devote himself to magic only. It was his work, his hobby, his life.

Houdini the aviator, about 1910. These machines were so fragile it does seem that it would take a magician to fly one!

10

Escape from a Water Torture Cell

In 1912 Houdini returned to the United States to perform at Hammerstein's Victoria Theater. The Victoria was in the heart of Manhattan, on 42nd Street and Broadway. It was famous for its roof garden with a huge water tank.

Harry got an idea for improving his mystery box escape; he would escape from the box underwater. The large tank on the roof garden of the Victoria was just the place for such a stunt. To make it more exciting, he had two pounds of lead attached to the box. He called the stunt "My Challenge to Death."

For Harry it was as simple as his first mystery box escape. But to the audience it seemed like the most dangerous and difficult trick they had ever seen. There were wrestlers, bicycle riders and men with seventeen foot beards on the program. But Houdini's act received the greatest applause.

Escape from a Water Torture Cell

Harry asked that his first week's salary of $1,000 be given to him in gold. Carrying his heavy load, he hurried home. Cecilia Weiss was sitting at an upstairs window as Harry came near. He waved to her and hurried up the stairs.

Arms and legs chained, Houdini is about to enter a box which will be sealed, cast into the river — and from which he will escape.

"Mother, hold out your apron." He opened the bag. As her eyes opened wider and wider, he poured a river of gold into her lap.

"I promised on the Torah that I would take care of you, Mother." The love he had for her shone in his eyes. Mrs. Weiss took her son's face in her hands and kissed him gently on both cheeks.

One afternoon Harry stopped in at the headquarters of the Neckwear Makers Union. He had once been a member of the union. He was glad to meet a co-worker from Richter's necktie factory. The man greeted him. "Ehrich, you know the greatest escape you ever made? It was from the neckwear business." Both men laughed.

When Houdini learned that competitors were copying his milk can escape, he was angry, but not for long. There was no time for anger. Instead, he improved his stunt. He also gave it a new name: the Water Torture Cell Stunt.

Instead of a milk can, he would stand upside down in a large mahogany cabinet lined with metal. One side of the cabinet was made of heavy glass. The top, which was moveable, had two small holes. The top was taken off and Harry's ankles were locked in the holes. His hands were fastened with handcuffs. He was lifted into the air and then lowered head first into the cabinet that was filled with water. With his feet in the holes, the top was fastened in place with padlocks. Through the glass side the audience could see Houdini hanging in the water, head down — feet up, waving goodbye as the curtain drew around the cabinet.

The audience waited breathlessly as the orchestra played *The Diver*. Three minutes later, the cabinet was still locked but Harry was free. The audience applauded wildly.

The Water Torture Cell escape became his most famous trick. How he did it no one knows. It was a secret he never revealed.

Another stunt that Houdini made more dangerous and exciting was his escape from a straitjacket. On a busy street in Washington, D.C., Harry, wearing a straitjacket, was tied at his feet to a crane and hoisted high above the sidewalk. As thousands of people stretched their necks to watch, he dangled upside down. In two and a half minutes, he had pulled the jacket down over his head and dropped it to the ground below. The crowd on the street was stunned.

Houdini sailed back to Europe for another series of performances. He and his mother stood on the dock, hugging and kissing each other in farewell, tears in their eyes.

On July 17, 1913 Houdini was performing in

*Houdini suspended in a straitjacket,
Washington, D.C., January 12, 1922.*

*Closeup of Houdini escaping from a
straitjacket while suspended in air.*

Denmark when he received a cable from Theo that their mother had died. He fell unconscious. When he was revived he sobbed uncontrollably. He had to see his mother before she was buried. He sent a telegram to Theo to delay the funeral until he arrived.

As Bess packed and made arrangements to return, she tried to comfort her husband. But Harry could not be consoled. As Cecilia Weiss was buried, Harry felt that his life had stopped. He was unable to work for two months.

When he recovered, Harry returned to Europe to keep his engagements. A year later, in July of 1914, World War One broke out in Europe and Harry and Bess returned to New York. He had another thriller in store for America — the mystery of the brick wall.

The first-night audience at the Victoria Theater waited impatiently for Houdini to appear. With the spotlight on him, he came onstage confident, sparkling, smiling.

"Ladies and Gentlemen. Tonight, with your kind permission, I shall try to walk through a solid brick wall. As you can see, there are no trapdoors on the stage." But there was one that they could not see.

As the audience watched, a wide rug was spread on the stage. The workers proceeded to build an eight-foot brick wall reaching from the front to the back of the stage. On either side of the wall, they placed a screen facing the audience.

When all was ready, the orchestra struck up lively music. Harry went behind the screen on the left side of the wall. "Here I am!" he shouted, waving his hand. "Now I'm here!" he shouted a few seconds later, as he waved his hand above the screen — on the right side of the brick wall.

The audience had seen a solid wall being built. Then they had seen Houdini, first on one side, then, an instant later, on the other side. There was no way he could have gone around the wall or over it. They would have seen him. How was it possible?

Houdini had gone beneath it. Below the rug was the unseen trap door. As he walked over the rug, the trapdoor was opened by an assistant below the stage. The rug sagged just enough to make space for him to crawl under the wall to the other side.

If the audience was mystified, it was little compared to its wonder at the disappearing elephant. If other magicians could make pigeons and ponies disappear, Houdini would make an elephant disappear. The Hippodrome in New York had an enormous stage, just the stage for a huge elephant. So Harry borrowed an elephant.

Jennie was her name, and she weighed 10,000

Jennie, the disappearing elephant.

pounds. Dressed with a blue ribbon around her neck and a fake wrist watch on her leg, she was brought onstage by her trainer. "Jennie will now give me a kiss," he said. Jennie raised her trunk as if to kiss him, and Harry placed a lump of sugar in her mouth.

A huge black cabinet was wheeled onstage by twelve men. Houdini led Jennie into the cabinet. He drew the curtains closed. He drew them open. The elephant was gone!

To prove that the elephant had disappeared, the curtains in the rear of the cabinet were opened so that the audience could see right through. They could see no elephant there.

Actually the cabinet was not empty, the elephant had not disapeared. Jennie was lying stretched out along one side of the cabinet, with a black screen pulled in front of her. The black screen was like the black walls of the cabinet. With the combination of blackness and a bright spotlight at a distance from the audience, people thought they were looking at the entire inside of the cabinet.

In spite of Houdini's thorough preparation for a stunt, and the care he took to prevent accidents, there were times when things went wrong.

Once he got into a milk can filled with beer. Houdini never drank anything with alcohol. He was overcome by the fumes of the alcohol in the beer, and he had to be pulled out.

Another time he was chained and locked into the belly of an embalmed sea monster. The arsenic that was used to preserve the dead animal made him sick. He escaped, but with great difficulty.

But the most dangerous stunt — one in which he almost lost his life — was the one in which he had himself buried alive. It happened in California. His assistants dug a hole in the ground six feet deep and wide enough so that there would be air all around him. Confident that all would go well, he jumped in. Suddenly the earth began to fall and pile up on him. He found it hard to breathe. The weight of the earth was greater than he had expected. Terror gripped him. Frantically, he began to claw at the earth. More earth became loose and fell on him. He tried to yell for help. Earth filled his mouth. It filled his nose, his ears. There was only one thing he could do — dig and claw with all his strength. At last he saw a ray of light. The hands of his assistants pulled him from the grave. A moment more and he was above ground, exhausted, grateful to be alive.

11

No Escape from Death

In 1917 the United States entered World War One. Harry tried to help his country. He invented a device to help sea divers escape quickly from their heavy diving suits in an emergency. He gave it to the Navy, but it was never used. He sold war bonds. When soldiers came to see his shows in the theater, he invited them backstage and taught them how to escape from German handcuffs in case they were captured by the enemy. He also entertained soldiers in camps and hospitals. His favorite act, and the soldiers' favorite, too, was to pick $5 gold pieces from the air and toss them to the soldiers. Those who caught them, kept them.

Between theater work and war work, Houdini was busier than ever.

Also a new and exciting business was developing in the United States — the moving picture industry. It caught Harry's imagination. Harry Houdini, magician, went to Hollywood and became Harry

Houdini, movie actor. He jumped off bridges and climbed tall buildings before a camera. Nothing was too hard for him. But when it came time for him to kiss the beautiful woman he had just saved from falling off the edge of a steep cliff, or another dangerous place, he couldn't do it. He could kiss only one woman, he said, his beloved Bess. His movie career ended quickly.

Now there was something more important that he had to do. Ever since he had seen a spiritualist perform at the Chicago Fair, he had become interested in the subject of spiritualism. Spiritualists,

Harry Houdini, movie star, being attacked by cannibals. Does he escape? What do you think?

sometimes called mediums, claim that they can make the forms of dead people appear, or carry messages to and from those who have died.

During his early years, when he and Bess had been out of work and were hungry, he had taken a job acting as a medium. On a darkened stage he rang bells and made shadowy faces while figures appeared in the dark. He pretended that he was talking to dead relatives of people in the audience. A "spirit" voice answered him. Only Harry knew that it was the voice of Bess.

After his mother's death, Harry met a medium who claimed that she could help him communicate with his mother. In his great sadness, he wanted to believe he could contact her. But when the "message" from his mother came in English, he knew the medium was a cheat. His mother had never learned to speak or write English.

After the war, many parents whose sons had been killed were paying mediums to bring "messages" from their dead boys. Harry felt that he must tell what he knew about such mediums. He went on a speaking tour. These mediums were fakes, he said. They used tricks that fooled people. Anyone could talk to the dead, but the dead couldn't answer, he told his audiences. He gave demonstrations of the tricks mediums used and urged people to have nothing to do with them.

Harry Houdini had become rich and famous. But he always remembered what it was like to be Ehrich Weiss selling newspapers on freezing winter days on the street corners of Appleton, Wisconsin. And he always remembered that there were still people who were cold and hungry. Especially children.

One cold wintry day the Houdinis were walking on their way to the theater through the poor section of Edinburgh, Scotland. Barefoot boys and girls were playing on the streets. Bess gripped Harry's arm. "Look, Harry. They're blue with cold. We've got to do something for them."

"We will, Bess. We will," he answered. He walked on without saying a word the rest of the way.

The next day Harry and Bess bought 300 pairs of shoes and put a notice in the newspapers inviting children who needed shoes to come to the theater. Hundreds came, but there were more children than there were pairs of shoes. When all the shoes were fitted, Harry took the remaining children to the nearest shoe shop. Every child who had come to the theater that day walked home with a new pair of shoes.

Harry put on a show for children without parents. He entertained in prisons and hospitals. He was concerned about old people, especially magicians who were too old to work. In London, he contributed money to build a hospital for elderly actors and magicians.

His acts of charity were never reported in the newspapers. He didn't want that kind of publicity. It was in the Jewish tradition, he said, to give charity quietly.

In the Fall of 1926, Houdini was performing in Montreal, Canada. One evening he was invited to speak to the students at McGill University. A few days later, several students came to interview him in his dressing room at the theater.

"Mr. Houdini, you have stated that you can tighten the muscles of your belly so that if someone punches you, you will not be hurt," one student began.

Houdini nodded. He was lying on a couch, looking through his mail.

"Do you mind if I take a few punches?", the student asked.

Houdini was busy reading an important letter. Without looking at the speaker he nodded again, his mind on his letter. The young man, strong and six feet tall, then gave him three hard blows to the stomach. Houdini was taken by surprise. He had not had time to tighten his muscles to protect his insides.

After the students left, Harry went about his work. That afternoon he felt pain but he said nothing to Bess because he was sure she would call a doctor. Harry had no time for a doctor. That evening he would be giving his closing performance in Montreal. Then he would be going to Detroit, where he was booked for a show. Besides, he was sure that what he felt was only a muscle pain.

When Harry returned to his hotel that night, the pain was so bad he couldn't sleep. Bess massaged his stomach. She wanted to call a doctor, but Harry refused.

The next day they left for Detroit. On the train he could no longer bear the pain. Bess pleaded with him to let her get help. Finally, he consented.

Upon his arrival in Detroit, the doctor examined him. "Acute appendicitis," he said. "You must go to the hospital at once."

"With a full house waiting for me?" Harry replied quickly. The show was to open that night.

With a fever of 104 degrees, Harry Houdini began his performance. But he never finished. He had to be carried off the stage.

His appendix had ruptured when the student had punched him. He was operated on several times within the next few days, but it was too late to save his life.

With his beloved Bess and his brother Theo at his bedside, he whispered, "I'm tired of fighting," and closed his eyes — forever. It was October 31, 1926 — Hallowe'en.

Index

110

111

112